Ananda: Discover The Vedic Way to Happiness & Bliss

Ananda

DISCOVER THE VEDIC WAY
TO HAPPINESS & BLISS

LISSA COFFEY

Foreword by Dr. Suhas Kshirsagar

Bamboo Entertainment, Inc

For every soul that is seeking,
May this help you see.

TABLE OF CONTENTS

FOREWORD

Ananda: The Vedic Way to Happiness & Bliss is a wonderful book from my dear friend and colleague Lissa Coffey. I have always admired her devotion, clarity and ease with which she distills some of the complex Vedic principles in simple steps for Mindful Living.

Happiness is just a state of Mind. Happiness is something everyone desires, yet how we find happiness is still a mystery. Finding happiness is the purpose of every other purpose in life. Many people believe that they will be happy if they have money, good relationship or being healthy but in fact these are just the byproducts of happiness not the actual cause. When we are happy, it leads us to all of these things.

From a Vedic perspective, the goal of human life is the expansion of happiness (ananda). If we learn how to maintain the inner calm in the midst of the turbulence of life then we are more likely to find everlasting happiness. It is the most natural state of pure existence.

When we have explored and exhausted all the tools that brings us momentary happiness, then the only path left is the road to enlightenment. We transcend the limitations of our senses to connect with our cosmic self. Your immortal self, which is untouched by the challenges of life, is the abundant reservoir of non-sensorial bliss. Here you are more likely able to find fulfillment, peace, joy and true happiness that nobody can take away from you.

We all want to be happy and maintain this state permanently, but we can't depend upon external circumstances for lasting happiness. It has to come from inside out. The Vedantic Wisdom and the modern medical research are finally converging at this point of positive psychology. I can't think of any other universal need than finding true happiness. Ancient Vedic literature has described non-sensorial happiness as the first step to attain everlasting peace and bliss.

In fact, regardless of your external circumstances, you can still experience a deeper, permanent state of happiness. When we look at list of the happy countries in the world, it features many poor countries at the top. It is not only about material prosperity. It is all about mental conditions, attitude and your upbringing. If you start leading your life from the inner state of joy and equanimity then you simply attract splendor & abundance. You start radiating happiness in every area of your life.

From a Vedic perspective the human mind is happy when it gets what it want and unhappy when it does not get what it wants (Anishtasya Labhat, Ishtasya Alabhat). The most important piece of the puzzle is a Stable Intellect, which effectively regulates mind, sensory faculties and also helps us transcend our ego. When the mind and senses are directed inwards, it is Yoga, when it is directed outwards it leads to Bhoga (insatiable desires) and Roga (diseases).

In other words, our inability to differentiate between actual and perceptual is the main cause of suffering. Our senses are gateways of perception and the way we learn to experience the world is exactly the main reason why we suffer from a roller coaster of emotions. The most fundamental emotions are Sukha (happiness) & Dukha (Unhappiness). The Sanskrit word Kha means Akasha or Space. When the things are flowing it is Sukha and when the flow is obstructed, it is Dukha. Objectively speaking if you are happy you are more likely to be healthy. Health, Heal, Whole and Holy simply suggest the process of healing from inside out.

The Vedic template for everlasting happiness includes Body Awareness, Detachment (vairagya), living mindfully, sensory regulation and a pursuit of enlightenment. We are a mere reflection of collective consciousness. It simply boils down to the golden rule that you must give others what you want for yourself. Spontaneous fulfillment of desires often comes from pure intentions and community well being. If you are surrounded with happy people you are more likely become a happy soul.

Once again, I welcome you on the wonderful journey with Lissa Coffey in exploring Ananda. She explains a practical approach to happiness based on Vedic Wisdom. Lissa has a unique way of translating ancient wisdom for modern audience, and showing her readers how to apply these important principles to their lives. If you are looking to find bliss, just by finding this book you've made a great start. Take Lissa's words to heart and you will surely discover the bliss that resides in you and in each one of us.

Be Happy!

Dr. Suhas Kshirsagar BAMS MD (Ayurveda)
Author: Hot Belly Diet
Director: Ayurvedic Healing Inc.
Faculty/Consultant: Chopra Center, CA

INTRODUCTION

We all want to be happy, right? No matter where you live, what you do, or which religion you practice, happiness is a universal quest, something we all consider important in our lives. There have been scientific studies about it, many documentary films have covered the topic, and countless books have been written about just how to attain happiness. And yet, somehow, for many, happiness remains elusive.

How do we "get" happy? We seemed to have figured out what doesn't work. We know money can't buy happiness, as we've seen many rich people who are totally miserable. We know that power and success don't necessarily come with happiness. Many people in positions of power are under a huge amount of stress, which can lead to health problems, mental, physical and emotional. We also know that we can't borrow someone else's happiness. Sometimes, when someone we know is happy we might even feel worse about our own situation because we see the happiness that we are missing. And we know the "if, thens," or the "when, thens" definitely don't work. We can't postpone happiness – if we're going to be happy, we need to be happy now – not if or when we get something or something happens to us. It seems we are constantly pursuing the goal of happiness rather than just being happy.

Some people say that the root of unhappiness is in desire. And if we can just give up our desires we will be happy. They say that when our desires are unfulfilled we are unhappy. And then when our desires are fulfilled, we are again unhappy because we are afraid of losing that object of desire. And besides this, new desires are constantly creeping up on us. No sooner do you get your new smart phone, the one you've saved up for and waited for, than a new version comes out that is even better, even smarter! We can't possibly keep up with it all.

So maybe giving up our desires is an answer to finding happiness? Nope. Suppressing our desires also makes us unhappy. We can't help what we want. We're living in a material world – self-denial is both unnatural and unrealistic. Indulging all of our desires doesn't work either – self-indulgence can lead to addiction, which not only makes us unhappy, but can also basically ruin our lives.

Others say that to be happy we need to escape the world. But how can we do this? We have to earn a living and we want to contribute to society. Living on a mountaintop and meditating isn't convenient, or practical for most of us. As humans, we have needs that need to be met. We have relationships that are of value to us that need to be nurtured. And we've developed a fondness for indoor plumbing and electricity, both of which cost money. So escaping the world is not the way to happiness, either.

Vedanta, the ancient wisdom from India that has become a philosophy for living, says that happiness is a state of mind. It is a state of mind where we have peace of mind, and we know who we are, we know our true Self. Vedanta explains that we can make our minds tranquil through discipline, knowledge, and training.

The opposite of a tranquil mind is a restless mind, and Vedanta says that a restless mind, not desire or anything else, is the root of all unhappiness.

And of course, in this hectic world we live in, we are susceptible to having a restless mind! First all the technology that keeps us plugged in, our computers, smart phones, TV, video games, apps – we've got something vying for our attention at all times, 24/7. We are reachable by phone, text, e-mail, social media – so there's an ongoing conversation that we're a part of, and we often feel left out if we don't participate. Then we've got all the desires that arise from living in a material world. We feel like we have to keep up – we see the next, new car in a commercial, or in our neighbor's driveway, and we can't help but be somewhat impressed and maybe even want one for ourselves.

We've got all the usual attachments that keep our mind restless as well. We're attached to our job, our home, our friends, our families – we worry when things aren't going well, we strive to make things better. We're attached to all the things that we have – we spend money on closet organizers and storage facilities – we often have to park our cars outside because the garage is filled up with so much of our stuff that we just can't let go of. All of this requires physical space but also mental space as well. How do we keep track of it all?

And then there are our human urges that cause the mind to be restless. We need to eat. What are we going to have, when are we going to have it, where are we going to eat, how are we getting there, how are we paying for it, what about our food allergies... there are ongoing thoughts about any and every urge we have.

The restless mind robs us of peace, and without peace, we can't have happiness. However, Vedanta says that the restless mind can be brought under control with self-awareness. And how do we do this? By deepening our spiritual consciousness. By being our true Self – because the true Self is the source of all peace and happiness.

The restless mind takes us further away from knowing who we really are, and living and expressing as our true Self. The tranquil mind brings us closer to knowing who we are, and helps us to live and express ourselves as our true Self.

The restless mind is made tranquil through discipline, knowledge, and training. Yes, discipline, self-control, self-awareness, meaning it is indeed up to each one of us to do this for ourselves. We need to be mindful of our thoughts, words, and actions. We need to learn and understand the laws of the universe. In attaining knowledge, we need to use both faith and reason. We need to develop self-understanding. We need to become spiritually mature. It takes practice. And Vedanta shows us exactly how to do this. And that's what this book is all about. I'll give you all the tools you need to get started so that you finally find the happiness, that beautiful bliss that you've been looking for, and more.

Vedanta says that it is our goal in life to not only to be happy, but to also be free. Liberation in Sanskrit is called "jivanmukti" – this is freedom while living in the body. Free from a restless mind, free from suffering, free from sorrow. Jivamukti is realizing our true nature as pure and divine in the midst of this crazy and chaotic world we live in.

This liberation is something that any of us can attain, something that each of us will inevitably attain as it is the destiny of all living beings. Vedanta says that we have multiple lives, and that we can achieve liberation now or at any time. It's up to us, really. Each of us alone is responsible for our own liberation. No one can do it for us. Not our parents, or our children, not our ancestors who have passed, not some magical guru. It's up to each one of us to do it for ourselves.

It starts with Self Knowledge. Self-knowledge is the direct perception of the One Self, living as the individual self in each and every one of us, and in all living beings. We can see this Self in meditation with our eyes closed. And we can see this Self in the visible world as we go about our daily activities. Self-knowledge is not selfish at all. On the contrary, when we see the divine in all beings, and we see how everything we do affects every one of us. We become more loving, more compassionate, more accepting, more kind. Self-knowledge changes us for the better, forever. And as we each change ourselves, the world becomes a better and better place for all of us.

Vedanta says that jivamukti, or liberation, brings us a deep happiness known as "anandakanda." Anandakanda means the root of bliss. Anandakanda is represented as a lotus in the heart center, where we feel bliss, love, and happiness. Nothing material, nothing limited, could possibly fulfill the desire for freedom or happiness. Only the spiritual can do that. We need to know the true Self.

CH. 1
What Do You Want?

*He or she who knows
that enough is enough
will always have enough.*

-Lao Tzu

Typically, when people are asked the question: "What do you want?" the answer is usually something along the lines of "to be happy." Many people also answer that they want to be healthy as well. And there is a direct correlation between health and happiness. Happy people tend to be healthier, and have stronger immune systems. It isn't a surprise that happy people are better at taking care of themselves as well. They tend to eat better, exercise more regularly, and go in for regular check-ups.

The answer is generally the same when people are asked what they want for their children. We want them to be happy. We know the value of happiness, and we know how much better life is when we feel happy, so we want that for our children as well.

To want happiness is a natural instinct. It's a part of life for all of us. Yet in this human existence happiness is not always so easy to come by. Life has its ups and downs. One of the basic tenets is that life is the co-existence of opposites. If we have happy, there has to be an opposite, so there is unhappy. Positive – negative. Good – bad. Calm – chaos. For every left there is a right. For every high there is a low.

Our lives are filled with uncertainty. We've got this physical body to deal with, and all the bumps and bruises and aches and pains that come along with it. We never know what is going to happen to us next. We have to cope with relationships, all these people in our lives.

We have to figure out all the money stuff – go to school – get a job – pay the bills – raise our kids. Life is uncertain, and often difficult.

Vedanta teaches us that for every problem we have, there is a spiritual solution. We can use the wisdom of Vedanta to help us solve the basic problems of life. We can experience life without worry, fear, or emotional extremes. We can be free from struggles, and experience bliss, or ananda. Ananda is a Sanskrit word that means bliss, peace, contentment, and happiness. It's that warmth in your heart where you know all is right with the world and you feel love. This is a balance, a middle path, but it's not complacency. Instead it's a calm, tranquil, peace of mind. It's a feeling of reverence, and gratitude.

So how much do we really want this? Let's look at where we are putting our attention. For many, our attention is divided into dozens of different broken shards and we are busily trying to get the pieces to fit together just right. We feel like our attention turns to one thing, and another thing suffers because of it. We can't physically be in two places at one time, but we have learned to multi-task, so that mentally we are in multiple places at any given time! No wonder we're stressed out.

Our attention has shifted away from the spiritual and towards the material. In the modern world, the acquisition of wealth is considered to be the measure of success. There is imbalance when we see the attention paid to the antics of celebrities versus the accomplishments of scholars who are working to better the world. Somehow "loving life" has come to mean spending money, accumulating designer purses, and driving exotic cars.

When we look at what is happening in the world today, and the statistics regarding depression, obesity, divorce, unemployment, and economics – it's easy to see that we are in a crisis. And really, it all boils down to the fact that we are in a spiritual crisis. It's like we're spiritual bankrupt, the account is overdrawn.

So, what do we do about this spiritual crisis? How do we build our account back up? We've looked outside of ourselves, and we know that doesn't work. It's time to turn within. Vedanta explains that all the answers we seek are inside each one of us. We start right where we are, with ourselves. Vedanta says that happiness depends on our peace of mind. Our peace of mind depends on our self-control, or discipline. And our discipline depends on our self-awareness, knowing who we really are.

UNIVERSAL PRINCIPLES

Vedanta is based on a set of universal principles. But understanding and following these principles we can find solutions to our problems, and have peace of mind.

Life is made up of the coexistence of opposites.

It is impossible to have one side without the other, like two sides of a coin. It is important for us to find a balance within the opposites, a middle path, and not let either extreme affect our outlook on life. So when we get caught up in one side or another, we can recognize that there is much more than just this – it's just the way life is. We can strive for balance, and not let the extremes knock us down.

There is an opposite for everything – left/right, up/down, male/female, Democrat/Republican, black/white… but the smarter we get, the more information we have, the more knowledge we garner over our years, the more we understand that these are two extremes, and that there is a LOT of room for the middle, for everything in between. Many, many shades of grey. Have you ever gone shopping for paint – seen all those little samples? Well, then you know – and there are even more than that.

Eventually, this "line" becomes more and more flexible, and we get past seeing the world as a coexistence of opposites and see it all as one. We see that this life isn't linear at all – it's not two sides, opposites, but a circle, not a coin, but a sphere, all connected, all one.

When we give up holding on to one side or the other, we become more flexible – we move more easily and can find our balance, the place where we feel most comfortable. We can express more fully who we are, and we feel more at peace, more content.

There is suffering in life.

This comes with the territory of being human. Suffering is not caused by bad luck, or by God, but by not knowing who we are, by feeling separate. We can overcome suffering with Self-knowledge. We can recognize and understand that everything happens for a reason, and look for a lesson in the experience. We can feel the pain, and at the same time choose not hang on to the suffering, but to learn from it and let it go.

There is a saying that pain is inevitable, but suffering is optional. We all go through things that are painful in life. And many times it is through these painful experiences that we learn the most. These are the times we get closer to knowing who we really are. When we can recognize these times as learning opportunities, we can get past the suffering more gracefully. We can even feel gratitude. When we feel grateful, we feel at peace.

Self-knowledge is our destiny.

This is the goal of human life, to learn who we really are. Every experience in life helps us to grow in this knowledge in some way. We can make Self-knowledge a priority in our lives and actively pursue it. We can become more awakened every single day just by living our lives in a mindful way. Living mindfully means paying attention, being aware, seeing beauty, unity, spirit in every one and every thing.

Just as a flower reaches towards the sun, our soul reaches towards Spirit. We can't help it. There is something in us that compels us to look for that something more, the one thing that will make us happy. We can try many different things, relationships, jobs, material items, vacations, and find that nothing works. Nothing outside of ourselves ever does work to make us happy. So then finally we decide to look within, to understand that we are the flower, and we are the sun. We finally discover who we are. Then we have self-knowledge; then we have that bliss that fills the heart.

We learn about spiritual truths through practice.

We can't just read books, or listen to talks, we need to experience truth for ourselves. We perceive this truth through the soul. To hone our perceptive skills we need to purify the mind with spiritual practices such as prayer and meditation.

There is beauty in ritual. We have so many choices to make every day. We have so many decisions that come our way, where we have to think, and weigh options. This brings us stress. But having rituals, good habits, frees us up. It's like picking out your clothes the night before an important interview. When you have one less thing to think about, worrying about what you are going to wear, then you can concentrate on more important things.

Meditation cleanses the mind. It helps us to think more clearly. It helps us to see, and feel, what is important in life. Just like brushing the teeth is good dental hygiene, meditation is good mental hygiene, and should be practiced every day, twice a day. It's checking in with Spirit, taking that time to feel the connection. We will see the benefits of meditation during our activity as we go about our day. Things just get a bit easier, calmer, we handle stresses better.

We know we have discovered who we really are when our character has transformed. We become more kind, compassionate, and loving because we understand that everyone is suffering on some level. We seek to help others, and in turn we find that we are helping ourselves as well. All of this brings us closer to understanding our true nature.

Human nature is essentially divine.

We are born to search for truth, we are compelled to seek liberation. We have gotten distracted from this search by the quest for success, power, pleasure and material things. But this goes against our true nature, and that is the cause of our suffering. We can make choices for where we put our attention, and how we spend our time and energy.

We are faced with choices for where to put out attention, and how to spend our time every moment of every day. Even on TV, look at how many channels we have to sort out. There are so many that we need a directory to figure out what is on when and where. Life is the same way, so many different channels – and we get to pick! It's this vast menu, an endless buffet. So where do we indulge? Do we watch the mindless shows, or shows that fill us with confusion, or rage? Or do we use this tool to obtain more knowledge, to see examples of what is possible? Do we eat the fast food without thinking, and end up bloated and uncomfortable? Or do we choose wholesome foods to nourish the body so that we are healthier, and we have more energy to focus on what is good for ourselves and for the world we live in.

Like children, we want to have more toys, to be the boss, to goof around. But eventually we grow out of this. It might take some of us longer than others, but as we mature spiritually we start to see what is really good for us, what benefits us, and we move towards that. When we experience the bliss of self-knowledge we have no more need for toys. Life is simple, and profound, and rich beyond measure.

There are four aims, values, or purposes of life:
Dharma: righteous conduct. This is moral sensitivity. We are human beings, not mere animals, and we need to look out for one another and not be selfish. We are all connected, we are here to help each other. This Dharma is behaving in a mature manner, keeping in mind our connection with others, understanding our purpose here in this lifetime.

Artha: acquisition of wealth. We often take this to mean material fulfillment, but it really means using just what we need, not being greedy. The real source of wealth is in spiritual fulfillment. When we have this all our needs are met. We understand that we have everything we need. Instead wanting more, we become more generous, sharing more. We understand the value of things, and what real wealth is. There's a country song with a lyric that says: "I've never seen a hearse with a trailer hitch." We come to learn what is important, and what we take with us. We learn what really makes us happy.

Kama: fulfillment of legitimate desires. We need to be able to express ourselves, to do what we love, to help others, and to pursue our spiritual growth. These are legitimate desires and they are psychologically necessary for our spiritual awakening. We have talents and gifts for a reason, and we can use those gifts to help others. When we do, we feel good, happy, and free.

Moksha: freedom of the soul. This is only attained through Self-knowledge. Moksha give both purpose and meaning to the other three values of life. And at the same time, Moksha is the culmination of achieving Dharma, Artha, and Kama. When we are free we have unlimited knowledge, and boundless joy. What could be a better description of the kind of happiness we all want than "boundless joy?"

Knowing these four aims, or values of life helps us to make better choices in life.

All of creation is Pure Consciousness.

What does this mean? There is no beginning or end, no time or space. Time and space are man-made measurements. Knowing this helps us to differentiate between what is real and what is not real. What is real is everything that is beyond time and space, that has no beginning or end.

There are 25 qualities that make up this Pure Consciousness – this Unified Field of all there is. And the descriptions of the qualities illustrate the profound, infinite nature that we have access to: All possibilities, infinite creativity, infinite dynamism, infinite correlation. And also, Freedom, and Bliss. When we have self-knowledge, we understand that all the Universe is this, and as a microcosm of the vast universe, we are indeed this as well.

Everything that exists is connected.

Life is interdependent, not independent. All is One. This Oneness is the basis of all ethics and morals. Virtue is what unites us, and vice is what separates us. Knowing that we are connected to one another, how could we harm any living being?

One of my favorite quotes is from Pablo Casals, he said "You are a marvel. And when you grow up, can you then harm another who is, like you, a marvel? You must cherish one another. You must work – we must all work – to make this world worthy of its children."

There is an Ultimate Reality, and that is Pure Consciousness.

There is a Oneness to the Universe and everything in it is a part of it. Different religions put a variety names to this, but there really is no name. The Rig Veda says: "Truth is one: sages call it by various names." Knowing this we learn not to judge others. We're all going to the same place, and we will all get there eventually.

One of the qualities of Pure Consciousness is Self Referral. We learn to listen to ourselves, to decide for ourselves. We don't need to be swayed by anyone else's opinion. We don't feel any need to convince anyone of our opinion, and at the same time we don't feel the need to judge anyone on their particular way of doing things. We don't take things personally.

All faiths are in harmony.

Every religion is a different path to the same goal. There is a reason why we have so many different religions, and each religion is valid. We need to see the unity in our diversity. Problems arise between religions, and between people, when we forget the goal. We need to look at the big picture, the overall view of things, and not get caught up in dogma or politics.

How many degrees are there between East and West, or between North and South? Too many to count. Yet we can start at any point, move towards the center, and end up at the same place.

There is no one "right way." When we get caught up in thinking that our way is the only way, we are saying there is a right and a wrong. We're putting ourselves in a win/lose situation. And that's not how it is. Everyone's viewpoint is valid. We can learn to give up judgment and embrace acceptance. We can be open-minded, and open-hearted. And when we are, then we are happier.

Vedanta explains that greatness is measured by who you are, not by what you have, or by what you have done.

And that brings up our next question: *Who Are You?*

For Further Exploration

Think about what you want. Make a list, no rules, no limitations, just whatever it is that comes to mind include on this list. These things can be material or not – it doesn't matter. Just put it on paper.

Now take a look at this list. Is it short, or long? How long have you been wanting the things on this list? What is keeping you from getting the things on this list? Are there some things you have, but you just want "more" of?

Ask yourself why you want the things on this list. Is the perceived lack of these things causing you suffering? Ask yourself why you are experiencing this, and how you can shift your thinking so that you don't suffer.

Go deeper. Prioritize the things on this list. What is most important thing to you? What is most valuable? How do you feel about each of these things? What emotions come up when you read each work?

Put today's date on the list, and fold it up to refer to later. In about a month's time, after you've been practicing the principles in this book, make up another list, and compare the two side by side. See what has changed, or what you would like to see change.

Notes

CH. 2

Who Are You?

I have arrived. I am home.
In the here. In the now.
I am solid. I am free.
In the ultimate I dwell.

-Thich Nhat Hanh

When someone asks the question "who are you?" the response is typically that we give our name. That might be followed by where we live or what we do for a living. But is this who we are?

What's in a name? Our parents chose this name for us when we were born – and we've used it as an identifier ever since. But does it fit us? Do we know the meaning behind the name? Maybe you go by a nickname, or a name that you have chosen for yourself. But really, you are not your name, whatever that name is. The name is just a label.

We have many labels in this life:
Son/daughter   Sister/brother   Mother/father
Husband/wife   Aunt/uncle/cousin/niece/nephew
And then there are all the in-laws, steps, "ex"es and so forth.

Then we have the labels as we go through life:
Infant
Toddler
Child
Student
Teenager
Graduate
Job-seeker
Employed – *or whatever it is we do for work: chef, carpenter, entrepreneur, sales person, volunteer, etc.*
Retired
Elderly

And then there are the labels from groups that we identify with:

Girl scout

Lakers fan

American/ Croatian/ Indonesian, *or whatever nationality you have*

Californian – getting more specific down to the state or region you live in

Rotarian

Bruin *(for all those UCLA graduates our there) – or whatever mascot your school claims.*

Or even physical attributes that explain who we are:

Blonde/brunette/redhead

Then there are all the other affiliations, like:

Which political party we support

Which charity we serve

Any unions we belong to

And any groups you've joined, like a book club, or a bowling league.

On top of that we have our social media identity:

Which platform do you communicate through – facebook, twitter, instagram, pinterest – there are more and more of these every day. We have our face up on a webpage with a brief description that lets people know who we are in this particular arena.

I could go on and on, but you get the idea. While any of these titles or labels are descriptive, they don't even come close to explaining who we really are.

These labels are just illustrating roles that we play in this particular production of our life story. One role changes, and another begins. We can play multiple roles at the same time. We have different experiences and learn different things from each one. But whatever roles we choose to play, whatever hats we choose to wear or take off, the Real Self, the soul, remains.

Vedanta says that a human is a soul that uses the mind and body to gain experience. In other words, we are spiritual beings who come to this earth to learn and to grow. We are made up of the same "stuff" that the entire Universe is made up of. Ayurveda explains that this is air, space, fire, water and earth – and a soul. So we are a microcosm, a small representative of the whole, the macrocosm, the entire Universe.

The Soul, the Real Soul, called Paramatman, is the Self with a Big S. This is the Self that is also called consciousness, which is the "witness" of all things, the observer. If you take a moment to close your eyes and look within, ask yourself, who is doing the looking? That's the soul. That's you; that's who you really are.

Then there's this little s self, or non-self, or "apparent" soul that we are all so familiar with. This is called Jivatman, or the "embodied" soul. This is the "I" that we introduce when we meet someone. This is what psychologists call the ego, the experiencer of life and death, this is the you that is in quest of liberation.

Vedanta explains that no energy can be destroyed. It can however be changed, over and over again until it is eventually returned to its Source. How long does this take? It totally depends. For some things it could be a very short while, and for other things it could take thousands and thousands of years. We see this demonstrated in nature all the time. The tiny seed that over time grows to be a mighty tree. It catches a hold of the earth and digs its roots down deep, reaching towards the heavens. It takes years, decades, maybe even centuries, to reach its potential, and eventually, gradually, it starts to deteriorate. It shrivels up, it falls over, spent from having lived its life fully. It decays back into the earth. Meanwhile, its seeds have fallen, and taken hold. And the process begins again. Where does it begin, where does it end? It's the same tree, made up of the same stuff, but it is different, changed.

In nature everything goes from the subtle, the seed, or even the thought of the seed, to the gross, the tree, the producer of the seed, and back again from the gross to the subtle. On and on and on. As humans, a part of nature, the same thing happens to us.

The physical body goes through change. The physical body, made up of the five elements: air, space, fire, water, and earth, goes through a six step process of change during its lifetime.

Birth – the process of arriving into this world is indeed a big change.
Subsistence – after we've arrived, then we basically exist, we start living.
Growth – as time goes on we grow. The body physically gets bigger so that we can support ourselves and achieve interdependence.
Maturity – along with the growth, we mature. We don't just grow into bigger toddlers, we become men and women.
Decay – as we age, our body parts eventually get run down and worn out.
Death – at some point, the body itself fails to function enough to sustain life.

If the body were all there was to us, this could be a bit sad. But there is so much more to us than just the body! Vedanta says that we are made up of three bodies. Besides the physical body, we also have the "subtle" body – this is also made up of the five elements, but in their subtle form. The subtle body is expressed as our thoughts, memories and emotions. The subtle body is what continues after the physical body dies. And then we also have what Vedanta calls the "causal" body – and this is basically what we think of as the ego. It's what keeps us grounded in the physical, material world. We need all three of these bodies in order to fulfill all of our desires, both gross and subtle, in our lifetime.

And then beyond that, Vedanta says that the body is actually constructed with five layers, or "sheaths" called "Koshas." These are psychophysical layers that make up our individual personality. Let's take a look at these, starting from the outside and working inwards.

Annamaya Kosha. This is the outermost layer. It is our physical flesh and bone, our organs, blood, form, and coloring. This is all subject to change, it has a beginning and an end, so it is not the Real Self.

Pranayama Kosha. This is what animates us. It is also known as the "vital force." This kosha helps us to engage in physical activities, it makes the body appear to be living. However, this is not the Real Self, either, as Pranayama Kosha enters the body after conception, and leaves the body once the body dies. It takes place in space and time, it has a beginning and an end. But it is a vehicle for the inner self, and it is obviously important.

Manomaya Kosha is the mind. This operates on a subtle level and permeates both Annamaya Kosha and Pranayama Kosha. Through the mind we experience pain and pleasure. It allows us to think, believe, doubt, and react. The mind it a means to our freedom, but it also keeps us stuck right where we are. This is also not the Real Self, because the mind is unsteady, constantly thinking, constantly changing.

Vijnanamaya Kosha is the intellect. This is also on the subtle level, but the intellect is more refined than the mind. The intellect helps us to discern and discriminate. It distinguishes between any two things to determine what is desirable and what is undesirable. Here we have memories of past experiences, known as "samskaras." At the level of the intellect we can experience happiness or sadness with detachment. But this is not the Real Self, either. The intellect is subject to many different fluctuations, and ideas that come and go. The vital force, the mind, and the intellect all together make up the subtle body.

Anandamaya Kosha is bliss. This is where we experience happiness in varying, changeable degrees. And here we are closest to the Real Self – but still this is not the Real Self. The Real Self is changeless.

The Real Self is like that bright shining light beneath all of these five layers. We can't put it out. And this same light shines in each and every person. We need to see past these layers, through these layers, to experience the Real Self.

STATES OF CONSCIOUSNESS

So why don't we see this light all the time? Why don't we experience the Real Self every minute of every day? Well, because we're busy with the business of doing life. We spend much of our time in three states of consciousness: sleeping, dreaming, and waking. This is pretty much how we go about our day.

We understand sleeping. At this point our body is at rest, and our ego is basically unconscious. We don't really remember sleeping but we know it happened because it takes place in time and space. We need sleep for the mind and body to rejuvenate.

We understand dreaming. This state of consciousness is a little bit higher. We have images and ideas that come through – we can remember dreaming mostly, even if we don't remember the details. During the dream, it all feels real to us. But when we wake up, we understand that it was all a dream, not real at all.

And we understand waking. We think we are awake, as we walk around, go to our jobs, eat our food, talk to our friends and generally live our lives.

All of these three states of consciousness take place in space and time. And Vedanta says that while this appears to be our reality, it's not Reality, with a big R. All of this is just a play, an illusion, another dream. We are each actors in our own play. We have roles to play, but this isn't who we really are. While the ego might get caught up in all the work that needs to be done, the way people are treating us, the things that need to be fixed, the things we want but can't afford to spend money on, the Real Self is unaffected by all of it.

What we really need to do is to "wake up" and understand that our waking state, what we think is real, is not all there is. There is more.

That is not to say that our lives are unreal. Oh, they are very real. We are not imagining our suffering. We are not imagining our relationships, or our experiences. However, they also *aren't* "real" because they are temporary and circumstances and conditions can be changed. So what is going on here? It's called Maya. Maya is that veil of illusion that keeps us from the truth. Maya is not real or unreal, it just keeps us from seeing what is real. When we know to go beyond the veil of illusion, we can keep things in perspective, and know that there is more, there is always more to anything than what we can see. We can't fight Maya, we can't escape it – but we can overcome it with Self-knowledge.

BEING

Vedanta explains that there is another level of consciousness, beyond sleeping, dreaming, and waking – a 4th dimension to our personality, and that is called "Turiya," the omnipresent Consciousness, or "being." Turiya lets us experience and perceive what is Real. What is Real is the unchanging, that which exists beyond time and space. Turiya is also called the witness, or the Absolute. We find ourselves in Turiya when we meditate. In meditation we become unaware of our body. Our mind settles. We are unaware of time or space. We feel light, and peaceful. This feeling may be fleeting, as the mind does not want to be tamed. But we garner the benefits of Turiya nonetheless.

As we are in Turiya, we are the witness, we observe ourselves from that higher place. We know that we are more than the body. We feel the connection with all that is.

Sometimes we find ourselves in Turiya even when we're not meditating. When we are out in nature, maybe watching a beautiful sunset, or walking barefoot through the cool grass. We might find ourselves in Turiya when we are gazing into our child's eyes, or when we are dancing, or doing something we really love. These moments are precious. They are glimpses into the freedom and bliss that is available to us all the time. But we find them in the present moment. We find them by being, and by being fully present.

This is really feeling alive. It is a feeling of being yourself, being whole, being at peace. It's connecting with the Universe in that feeling of "I exist!" And yes, it's a celebration. If there is a formula for Self Realization it is this: **Sat Chit Ananda**. These three Sanskrit word mean: Knowledge (also Truth), Existence (also Consciousness), and Bliss. Keep this in your mind and heart and see how it feels. It's like stating: *"I am a part of all that is. I exist. I know that I am here on purpose, with purpose. This is the Truth. I am happy, joyful, content, and grateful to be right here, right now."*

MEDITATION

Meditation is a wonderful tool to help us experience Turiya. Vedanta says that meditation is the culmination of all of our spiritual practices, and goes beyond any religion or philosophy. It is for everyone. We don't need any special equipment; we just need to show up. During meditation, these are some of the experiences we can have:

-We become absorbed in the practice, and lose track of time.

-We lose awareness of our surroundings, and lose our sense of space.

-We lose our sense of ego, and feel our connection with Spirit, the Universe, all that is.

There are many different kinds of meditation, and you can choose which practice fits best for you. Vedanta says that the benefits of the practice will be greatest when you approach meditation with the right mood. Just as there are three egos, there are three states of mind, or moods. These are described using the the Gunas, or qualities: Tamas, Rajas, and Sattva. A Tamasic mood is dark, heavy, depressed. A Rajasic mood is restless and turbulent. And a sattvic state of mind, calm, tranquil and detached. This is the right space we want to be in. Some would call it the middle path. It's a place of balance and right thinking.

Vedanta says that we can sort of set the stage to have a sattvic mood and get the most from our meditation practice, and it gives us these tips:

-Provide favorable physical conditions. It is best to be indoors, away from elements such as weather, the wind, and more. We also want to feel safe while closing our eyes, and when we are outdoors we might be unprotected, and feel the need to stay more aware of our surroundings.

-Choose a healthy and positive place to live. You should be living in a space that feels like your home, surrounded by things that you love, that is clean and orderly.

-Choose a friendly, comfortable environment to meditate in. You might set aside a dedicated room for meditation, or a favorite chair.

-Choose a favorable time of day. The best times of the day to meditate are at sunrise and sunset, when the energies of nature are in line with a calm mind.

-Choose a style of meditation that fits with your personality. You should enjoy this time in meditation. It should be easy and comfortable for you.

-Have the right motive for your practice. Meditation is about growing spiritually, not about visualizing material items that you want or achieving worldly goals.

-Practice meditation on a regular basis. Set aside time twice a day.

In addition, there are other practices you can do in your activity that will help your meditation practice:

-Practice right speech. Watch the words you say. Speak only of what is true, pleasing and beneficial. Don't swear or gossip.

-Keep the company of those who are in alignment with your spiritual goals. It is good to have the support of others who want the same things in life. When possible, spend time with teachers and other people who are wise and who can share experiences with you.

-Eat food that is pure and fresh. Consider the benefits of following an ayurvedic lifestyle that includes an ayurvedic eating plan.

-Keep your spiritual goals foremost in your mind. Strive to learn and grow.

-Perform acts of service. Help others.

-Practice discernment. Learn to pay attention to what is real and what is not real.

-Listen to devotional music. Any music that moves you, that engages your emotions, and lets you feel closer to spirit, could be called devotional music. Music goes beyond words.

-Engage in chanting of the sacred texts. Learn mantras so that meaningful thoughts and words flow through your being.

-Practice pranayama, mindful, controlled breathing exercises.

-Practice japa, repetition of holy names, with mala beads.

-Engage in spiritual rituals. This could be lighting candles, saying prayers, writing in a gratitude journal, or anything that helps you feel closer to Spirit.

And here are a few of my own:

-Do what you love to do. Spend time in nature, even if it's just in your own backyard. Connect with the earth by going barefoot. If you have a special hobby that you love, spend time doing that.

-Nurture positive relationships. Spend time with people you love, and who love you. Laugh, have great conversations, have fun together. Get into the kitchen and cook together.

-Keep a daily routine. Ayurveda emphasizes how important this is to keep ourselves in balance. Get up with the sun and go about your day in harmony with nature.

For Further Exploration

Make a list of the labels you have been given, or have taken on. What roles do you play? What hats do you wear? How do you feel about these roles?

Picture your life as a movie, or a soap opera, or a situation comedy. Who are the supporting characters in your cast? How do they contribute to the script? How are you contributing to the script of their movies?

Observe yourself today. When you feel happy, step back and notice that feeling of happiness. Who is it that is feeling happy? Who is it observing the feeling of happiness? If you feel angry or upset, take a breath and observe these emotions and the energy that comes with them. What is your body feeling? Watch the energies pass through you. Don't try to squelch them, or deny them. Know that there is nothing bad about these energies and emotions, nothing to fear about them. Simply observe. Who is feeling this way? Who is observing the feeling pass? How does it feel to let them go?

Samskaras are stored energies or emotions. When we hold onto energy, these feelings can be triggered by similar circumstances. Try feeling the energy, observing it, and letting it go rather than storing it in the body to bother you later. Let it go. Empty yourself.

Set aside time for meditation. Find a time and place that work for you so that you can make this a part of your daily routine. Find the stillness. Observe yourself. Watch your breath. Who is breathing?

Notes

CH. 3
What Keeps Us From Feeling Happy?

Teach me your mood, O patient stars!
Who climb each night the ancient sky,
Leaving on space no shade, no scars,
No trace of age, no fear to die.

-Ralph Waldo Emerson

So, if we know we want to be happy, and we know what it takes to be happy, why are we just not feeling it?

There are a lot of reasons. We already discussed Maya. Maya is that veil of illusion that keeps us from seeing what is really real. It keeps us thinking that what we see, touch, hear, taste and smell is all there is to life. So there's that.

And then there's karma. Karma is basically habit. It's a conditioning of the mind where we habitually act in certain set ways. We cause ourselves suffering from our bad habits, and bring ourselves joy from our good habits.

Karma teaches us that every action has a reaction. The present is a result of actions from the past. The future will be a result of actions in the present. We can only take action in the present. So if we want to change our future, or our "fate" then we need to change the decisions we make, and the actions we take, right here in the present. We absolutely have free will. We don't need to continue with our bad habits – we can change in a moment, with just a thought, and with that change our entire future can change. In this way we can choose happiness by choosing actions in the present that will result in a joyful future.

If we've been making bad choices, getting into bad habits, then this could be why we are not feeling happy, or even suffering.

Vedanta says that suffering has three components to it:

Physical: This is from diseases, ailments, or injuries.

Mental: This is from depression, anxiety, or grief.

Spiritual: This is from a loss of faith, a feeling of hopelessness.

As we have learned by now, nothing material, no amount of money, no possessions however rare or desired, can ever eliminate suffering. Suffering is a part of human life. It is a part of the co-existence of opposites pair of pain and pleasure. But we can get past this roller coaster of emotions and find a way where we can not let suffering affect us, where we see suffering for what it is, and not let it ruin our life.

THE FIVE CAUSES OF SUFFERING

Vedanta explains that there are five causes of suffering:

Not knowing who we really are.
We have lost contact with Reality and we have bought into the illusion that all we can see, feel, hear, taste and smell is all there is to life.

Identifying with the ego.
We are attached to who we think we are. We have placed too much value and importance on things like our job title, our awards, or our bank account balance.

A deep attachment to the things we like.
This is a false sense of permanence. We don't understand that everything in this life is temporary – everything has a beginning and an end. At some point, everything started, and at another point, everything will end. The lifetime for a pencil is different than the lifetime for a house, but they both still have a beginning and an end.

A chronic aversion to the things we dislike.

This is a fear of change. We forget that change is necessary. When we feel uncomfortable or unhappy it is a signal to us that there is some imbalance, that a change is necessary. When we face it and do something about it we are better off.

Fear of death.

This is a stubborn clinging to life that does not let us move forward. To make it even easier to understand, Vedanta says that all five of these causes of suffering are contained in the first one – we suffer because we don't know who we really are. If we can just learn that – know it, feel it, live it, and then we won't suffer any more.

According to Vedanta, 50% of suffering comes from the external world. And 50% of suffering comes from us. We can't control what comes from the world. But we can control what comes from us. It takes contributions from both the world and from us to cause us suffering – so if we don't contribute, then that suffering never comes to us. We can control how we act, and how we react.

And why would we contribute to our own suffering? It comes back to habit again. We can't help it. Our ego takes over and we're not aware of the decisions we're making. The ego judges, it creates its own world and has an exaggerated sense of self-concern. The ego lives in Relative Reality. This is a reality that is real for a limited period of time – whether it is a few hours, days, months, even years. It appears to be real to us, but we know on a deeper level that there is more to it.

What we need to do is to connect with the Ultimate Reality. This is what is real for all time, always, everywhere. We are always connected with the Ultimate Reality, but we forget. It's like we have a cell signal, and we can communicate at any time, but we have the "hold" button pressed. When we forget that connection then all we see or hear is the Relative world and we think that's it.

The ego takes over and we get that "I, me, mine" mentality that is the cause of all of our misery. We get attached, we get selfish, and we get greedy. And we suffer because of it.

THE EGO

But ego itself isn't all bad. We need the ego to function in the world we live in. We don't want to obliterate the ego. But we can control it. Vedanta says that there are 3 kinds of ego. In Ayurveda we talk about the "gunas" or the "qualities" and these same 3 qualities apply to the 3 different kinds of ego:

The Infantile Ego

This ego has the qualities of "tamas" – it is weak, defensive and pessimistic. It is easily swayed by the opinions of others, and it runs away from problems.

The Adolescent Ego

This ego has the qualities of "rajas" – it is unsteady overly optimistic, and temperamental. It doesn't know what it wants. Instead of running away from problems it lashes out and is aggressive.

These two egos create suffering for us. These are "big" egos – they take up a lot of space in a room, and in our head. But there is another version of ego that actually helps us, there is a lot "less" ego in this one:

The Mature Ego

This ego has the qualities of "sattva" – it is self-controlled, purposeful and responsible. It is accepting of change, and can handle the stresses that come with life.

We'll talk more about ways that we can develop the mature ego in the next chapter.

Basically, what we need to know for now is that suffering keeps us from being happy, from being blissful.

And suffering comes from not knowing who we are, from losing contact with what is Real. So there is a solution to this, and that is spirituality. No material object can bring us the kind of joy that spirituality does. Fulfilling our material desires just creates more desires. Our material desires are insatiable. And this insatiability only creates more suffering for ourselves. Spirituality is the only answer. It's the only way to solve our suffering. Because when we know who we are, we know we already have everything we want, and we want everything we have. We know we are whole, complete and perfect exactly the way we are. We know we are love itself. And we have access to all the wisdom and beauty and grace in the Universe.

Vedanta tells us that if we want joy, we need to reduce our material desires.

If we want peace, we need to reduce the ego, develop a mature ego and let go of the infantile and adolescent egos.

If we want happiness we need to reduce our dependencies. We are self-sufficient, we need to simplify our lives, and stop relying so much on material objects. We need to maintain good physical health so that we can take care of ourselves. And we need to maintain good mental health by engaging in activities that are emotionally satisfying, like prayer, meditation, being creative, doing things we love.

We aren't just here for ourselves. Life is not independent; it is inter-dependent. We have a duty to help others. We are all connected. We need to recognize these bonds and overcome our selfishness and greed. It is our duty to contribute to the welfare of others, and when we do, we better understand that all existence is one. We feel good when we help others, because we are really helping ourselves. Swami Vivekananda said: *"They alone live who live for others, the rest are more dead than alive."*

Suffering comes with living a human life – but we can reduce suffer-ing and not have it affect us so much. One of the five causes of suffering is the fear of death. I've always heard that people are more afraid of public speaking than they are of death. But we can avoid public speaking – we can't avoid death – so maybe that is the reason why the fear of death causes us more suffering.

THE FEAR OF DEATH

Vedanta says that the reason we fear death is because we identify with the body, the physical body. And, as we have learned, Vedanta says that the physical body is just one aspect of the "whole" body. What we call "death" is the disintegration of the physical body. However, when the physical body disintegrates, the soul, and also the causal and subtle bodies, leave the physical body. Where do they go? It seems there is a kind of transition phase, where the soul experiences some kind of heaven or hell or learning situation based on the activities in that previous life. The time spent these is temporary. And then the soul must return again to earth to be born into another physical body.

The cycles of birth and death continue through many lifetimes, until we have finally achieved Self-knowledge. And Self-knowledge can only be achieved during our time on earth. The Baghvad Gita says: *"Even as the embodied Self passes, in this body, through the stages of childhood, youth, and old age, so does It pass into another body. Calm souls are not bewildered by this."*

When we achieve Self-knowledge, that is when it is said that we overcome death, we have reached immortality, meaning that we have moved beyond the cycle of birth and death. So at this point, having achieved Self-knowledge, whenever our physical body dies, we merge into the Oneness, where we find unbounded joy, immortality, and unrestricted awareness. We don't need to return to earth and experience human suffering any longer. At some point, all living beings will achieve Self-knowledge and liberation. It is inevitable for each of us. It's only a matter of time. And since there is no time or space in Spirit, that could be many, many, lifetimes!

Vedanta says that how we return to earth, and into what situation or circumstance we are born, is a result of how we lived our life, and also the thoughts that we have at the time of our physical death. So, live a good life, and think good thoughts! Have faith, and devotion, and live life with love.

You might recognize this process as reincarnation. This is a concept that is not limited to eastern religions. Reincarnation is also mentioned in the bible. In Matthew 11:14 Jesus identifies John the Baptist as the prophet Elias reborn: *"And if you are willing to accept it, he is the Elijah who was to come."* (NIV)

OVERCOMING FEAR

So how do we overcome these fears that cause us suffering?
Vedanta has answers to help us:

Understand that aging is a part of life.
And death is a part of life. Life on earth without death is incomplete. No age that we go through is any more or less important than any other age. We are born, we go through being infants, toddlers, children, teenagers, young adults, mature adults, older adults, elderly adults, and eventually the physical body gets worn out. We learn at each of these stages of life. We don't need to fear any stage. Better for us to embrace each stage, and learn all we can while we're in it, as each offers unique opportunities for growth.

Address anxieties.
The reason we feel anxious is because we have attachments to things. We don't like change; we often fear it. We fear uncertainty. But we need to understand that uncertainty is where so much growth happens! We can challenge ourselves to face our fears. To

let go of possessiveness, to let go of needing to be right, and open our minds and hearts to the many new and exciting experiences and opportunities that present themselves.

Practice non-attachment.

We don't have to be afraid of losing something, or someone. We've learned that material items don't, and can't possibly, give us lasting happiness, because they are temporary. If we don't lose them, or break them, or wear them out, we still can't take them with us after the body dies. This is not the same as being cold or insensitive, or even unsentimental. It just means that we are seeing a higher ideal in life. We are seeing Spirit, or God, in everyone and everything. We can love and appreciate that. We don't need to own it or possess it or even have it love us back.

Practice meditation.

During meditation we become unaware of the body – this helps us to see that we are more than the physical body. This helps us to understand that the physical body is a vehicle for our spiritual growth. We don't need to be attached to it, and obsess over every little imperfection. We can love our body, and take care of it so that it can carry us through our time here, giving us more time to achieve Self-knowledge.

Do good deeds.

All of the "stuff" that we accumulate in this lifetime will be left behind once the body passes away. But, all of the many memories of all the good deeds we have done will be left behind. Anytime we help someone, or work to make a positive difference, leaves an impact on someone else. Those memories really can change the world, but helping people to think differently about life, and making contributions to the world and to each other. If you are doing good deeds, then you don't need to fear that you have left nothing behind.

When we live life without fear,
when we are fearless, then it's easier
for us to be happy and blissful.

For Further Exploration

What patterns have you set up in your life? Where are you on auto-pilot? How can you shake things up to free yourself to see possibilities, and to make new choices?

What is your relationship with change? What is your experience with change? Do you like change? Change is a stimulus for growth. Sometimes growth is painful. But growth is always good. How do you deal with change? See what positive changes you can make today. What have you been avoiding? Go there; do that. Challenge yourself to make a change for the better somewhere in your life.

Can you identify where you are suffering? Can you identify ways to change that? Explore your options and choose actions that create happiness in yourself and in others. We feel pain in the heart, and we also feel happiness in the heart. How can you heal your heart today so that you are more free to experience ananda?

Listen to your self-talk. The mind is rarely quiet! But you can be the observer and watch those thoughts pass by. You can observe without getting your emotions involved. Relax, breathe, release. Be still, and just be.

Notes

CH. 4
How to Find Bliss

Let us live happily,
though we call nothing our own.
Let us be like God, feeding on love.

-Dhammapada

Now we know what we want. We even have an answer to the "Who are you" question, even if we haven't fully understood and lived it yet. We know what is keeping us from being happy, and how to overcome our fears. So now it's time to find happy.

Bliss is found in what Buddhists call "The Middle Path." Vedanta agrees. It's not in the extremes, it's in moderation, it's in balance. It doesn't come with the Infantile or the Adolescent Ego, it comes with the Mature Ego. The characteristics of the Mature Ego are that it is free from anxiety, free from dependence, free from attachment and aversion, tranquil, enlightened, and balanced. So, if we can work on developing a mature ego, then we are more likely to find and experience the bliss that we seek.

FOUR AREAS OF SELF-GROWTH

We can develop a mature ego by focusing on four areas of our self-growth:

Physical. We need to take care of the body. Are we making mature decisions as to our diet and lifestyle? Do we exercise regularly? Do we eat fresh, healthy foods? We we watch the quality and also quantity of foods that we eat? Do we seek medical attention when we need to? Do we practice preventive health care by visiting the dentist and doctor for regular check-ups? Ayurveda is India's 5,000 year old Science of Life, and it gives us practical recommend-ations for how to be healthy and happy. Learn your dosha, your personal Ayurvedic mind/body type, and follow the daily routine so that you can be the best version of yourself.

Mental. The mind is working all the time. We can't stop our thoughts. But can we control our urges and our impulses? Can we think about things, and make informed, intelligent decisions? Do we consider the consequences of our actions? Can we plan ahead? Can we reason through problems and find solutions? We need to develop good mental habits.

Moral. Are we selfish, or do we consider other people when we take action? When we have good morals, we are away of how everything we do affects others in one way or another. We have concern for all things in all actions. Morality is the backbone of spirituality. It is important for us to develop good morals and behave ethically in any situation or circumstance. We can't determine, or change, what anyone else does. But we do have control over our own responses and reactions. Choose wisely.

Spiritual. When we understand who we are, we understand who everyone else is. We see our connection, we see the Oneness. We find fulfillment in unity. We spend time nurturing this connection with prayer, meditation, japa, and other spiritual practices. We prioritize our time so that our practices and rituals are an important part of our day, not something to be squeezed in around work, or the first thing to be cut from the schedule of a busy day.

Mature living helps us to understand that everyone is just doing the best that they can. It helps us to let go and forgive people who have harmed us, whether they have hurt us intentionally or not.

THE TWO MONKS

There's a story about two monks who were traveling together by foot. They had taken vows that they would never touch a woman. When they reached a stream, they found a woman who was stranded on one side – she was having trouble crossing the stream. The first monk, without hesitation, helped her out. He picked her up and carried her across. She was very grateful. Then the two monks went on their way. But a few miles into their journey, the second monk stopped and scolded the first monk: "How could you touch that woman? You took vows, that was not the right thing to do." The first monk was surprised at the heated emotion coming from his traveling companion. He said to his friend: "All this time you have been thinking about this? I put the woman down at the side of the stream, and yet you've been carrying her with you the whole way." When we are operating with a mature ego, we can let things go, and not hold on to grievances.

Mature living also helps us to understand that everyone makes mistakes. We can forgive others, and ourselves, for the mistakes we make knowing that these mistakes help us to learn and grow. Mistakes are a part of life, and they help make us who we are today.

The song from the movie Frozen, "Let It Go," is very popular, and I think it is because the lyrics resonate so much with so many people. We all need to learn to Let It Go! It's better not to hold on to grudges, it's better not to hold on to old, worn out items, it's better to just let go of anything in life that is not serving you in the best way possible.

Through mature living we learn that goodness and purity is our true nature. There is goodness in every one of us. The exterior may show otherwise, the good may be hidden behind masks, and acts of desperation, and lack of knowledge. But we don't have to fear anyone, or have an aversion to anyone, because we are all connected, we are really sharing this life experience with each other.

We also learn that desire is the cause of evolution. When we want things to be different, we take action to create change. In this way, one by one, we are making the world a better place. We have will, and we can make the changes we need to be happier in some way. When we strengthen our will, we strengthen our character.

With mature living, we can control our busy, automatic thoughts by asserting our spiritual thoughts. In this way our Higher Self controls the mind so we make better decisions.

DISPASSION

With mature living, it is easier to practice what Vedanta called "dispassion." Dispassion is a neutral state, a place of balance. We don't have to take sides, one way or another. This helps us to deal with our urges and impulses. It helps us to be more thoughtful. This gives us mental strength, so that we don't accumulate more than we need, and we don't accumulate all this stuff that we can't take with us.

As an example, we all get emails, and often we subscribe to catalogs from online stores. I don't know about you, but when I get an announcement about some sale they're having, with some ridiculous discount, maybe 70% off, and then there's a photo of a really great pair of shoes, I want to click on it! That's an urge. But I don't have to take action. I don't have to let that urge get the best of me. I can know that I have plenty of shoes in my closet and click the delete button.

Dispassion also teaches us that although we have free will, our will is not absolutely free. We can't have everything we want. We need to be discerning, and make good choices.

Mature living is about being aware, being mindful, living a full life. It helps us to live fully present, in present moment awareness. We are not regretting decisions from the past; and we're not haunted by what has happened to us in the past. At the same time we're also not worried about the future, or dreaming about what is to come for us. Instead we're living in the present, and putting our attention right where it should be.

SPIRITUAL AWAKENING

Once we've come to a place where we are living maturely, where we have had that moral and ethical awakening, then we are ripe for a spiritual awakening. When our spiritual consciousness is awake, it means that we are eager for the realization of Truth. We are that much closer to being free.

Vedanta says that a spiritual awakening is an awakening of the soul. At this point we see the Truth, the Absolute. We have direct perception of the Truth not through the mind's eye, but through the soul's eye. We have to get to this point all on our own. No one can gift it to us magically.

The Yoga Sutras explain that in our being we have six centers of spiritual consciousness. These are known as "chakras." We have an additional chakra at the top of the head. We actually have many more chakras, but these main chakras are the centers of spiritual consciousness. Kundalini is the coiled up, spiritual power that lies dormant in all living beings. Kundalini has been described as a sleeping snake, and it is awakened through our spiritual practices and disciplines. When Kundalini is awakened it moves up the spine, stimulating the chakras and awakening them, one by one over time. This helps us to heal, to move closer to spirit, to deepen our spiritual experiences.

Sahasrara
mantra: OM
modern color: violet
traditional color: pure light (a combination of all colors)
qualities: wisdom, liberation

Anja
mantra: OM
modern color: indigo
traditional color: white
qualities: clarity, reasoning

Visudda
mantra: HAM
element: space
modern color: blue
traditional color: smoky purple
qualities: calm, truth

Anahata
mantra: YAM
element: air
modern color: green
traditional color: scarlet flame
qualities: peace, harmony, love

Manipura
mantra: RAM
element: fire
modern color: yellow
traditional color: dark rain clouds
qualities: knowledge, discernment

Svadhisthana
mantra: VAM
element: water
modern color: orange
traditional color: orangey-red
qualities: joy, faith, confidence

Mulhadhara
mantra: LAM
element: earth
modern color: red
traditional color: red
qualities: vitality, vigor, growth

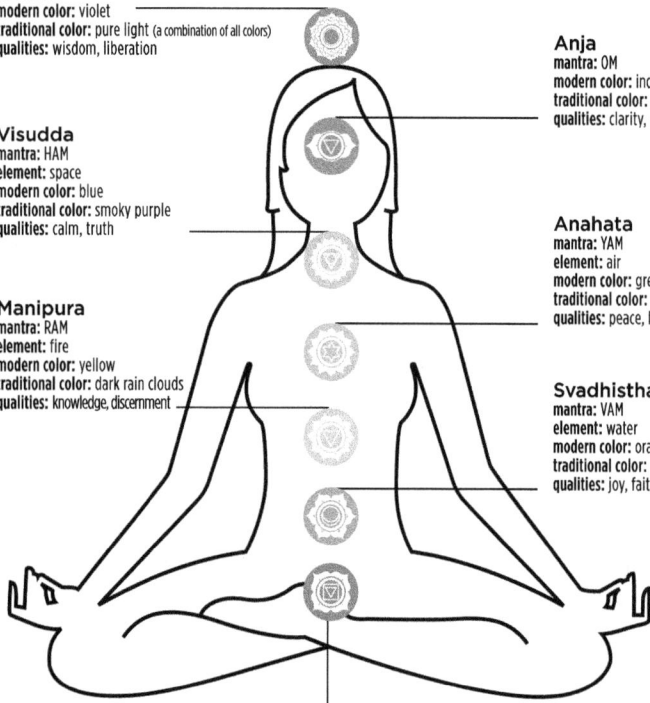

The first chakra is known as the Root chakra as it is at the base of the spine. It is called *Muladhara* and it is governed by the element of earth, "prithvi" in Sanskrit. It is represented as a lotus with 4 petals that is crimson, or deep red, in color. The four petals represent the four functions of the psyche: the mind (Manas), intellect (Buddhi), consciousness (Chitta) and ego (Ahamkara). Muladhara activates our memories of the past. This chakra is also the foundation for the development of our personality. The mantra for Muladhara is "LAM." We can stimulate this chakra by chanting LAM. This helps to bring out the positive qualities of Muladhara: vitality, vigor, and growth.

The second chakra is known as the Sacral chakra, and it is below the belly button, in the lower portion of the abdomen. It is called *Svadhisthana*, which translates to "own abode." Its color is vermillion, an orangey-red. Although over the years we have come to associate the colors of the rainbow with the chakras, Vedanta attributes its own color system with them. The Svadhistana lotus has 6 petals representing the negative qualities that we must overcome: anger, hatred, jealousy, cruelty, desire, and pride. This chakra is governed by the element of water, or "apas" in Sanskrit, a symbol of hidden danger. Water is life-giving, and soft. Yet when out of control water has an immense power. When negative emotions move from the subconscious to the conscious, it can shake us off balance. Awakening this chakra helps us to overcome our impulses and urges. The positive qualities that come out of Svadhistana include joy, faith, and self-confidence. The mantra for Svadhistana is VAM.

The third chakra is known as the Solar Plexus chakra, and it is located right behind the belly button. Its name is *Manipura*, which means "City of Jewels." This chakra is symbolized as a lotus with 10 petals. The 10 petals represent the 10 vital forces, or Pranas. To reach this level of consciousness we must first overcome the negative qualities of Svadhistana. The Manipura Chakra holds many beautiful jewel-like qualities such as knowledge, wisdom, discernment, and clarity. Awakening this chakra helps us to become self-aware. The element associated with this chakra is fire – and the fire in the belly that helps with digestion, and also ambition, is called "agni" in Sanskrit. When Manipura is strong and enlivened, digestion is strong, and our health is good. In modern times we see this chakra as yellow, but in Vedanta, its color is described as that of dark, heavy rain clouds. The mantra for Manipura is RAM.

The fourth chakra is commonly called the Heart chakra. In Sanskrit, this chakra is known as *Anahata*. It is located in the heart center of the chest. Anahata is symbolized by a lotus with 12 petals representing the 12 divine qualities of the heart: bliss, peace, harmony, love, understanding, clarity, purity, unity, compassion, kindness, forgiveness, and empathy. The corresponding element for Anahata is air, called "vayu" in Sanskrit. Air helps our consciousness to expand. At this level of consciousness we have meaningful spiritual experiences. When this chakra is awakened, we experience positive emotions that express as Bhakti, pure, divine love and devotion. It helps us to overcome confusion, desire, jealousy and despair. We have come to recognize the fourth chakra as the color green, but Vedanta describes Anahata as a scarlet flame. The mantra for Anahata is YAM.

The fifth chakra is familiar to us as the Throat chakra. In Sanskrit it is called *Visudda*, meaning purity. It is located in the center of the throat. Visudda has a lotus with 16 petals, representing the potential abilities that we can develop as humans. The throat is where sound takes place, so the sixteen petals of the lotus also represent the sixteen vowels of the Sanskrit alphabet. In modern times we see the Throat chakra as blue, but Vedanta sees Visudda as a smoky purple color. The element for Visudda is space, or Akasha. The fact that space is in the throat reminds us that it is through our breath that we purify the body, and also the mind. Think about how when you might feel angry or confused and you just need to take a deep breath to clear your mind and feel better. Think about how we tend to "swallow" negative experiences, and how this affects us until we can face our problems, and resolve them. When Visudda is awakened we have a clear voice, we speak our truth, we are able to express ourselves, our abilities and skills shine through. We also experience a certain amount of spiritual absorption, spirituality becomes very important in our lives. Developing this chakra helps us to overcome anxiety, and feelings of being stuck. The mantra for Visudda is HAM.

The sixth chakra is often called the Third Eye chakra. In Sanskrit it is known as *Ajna*, and it is located in the middle of the forehead, between the eyebrows. Ajna means knowledge. This chakra is symbolized by a lotus with two petals, indicating that at this level of conscious there is only the Self (Atman) and God (Paramatman). In modern times we see this chakra depicted as the color indigo, but in Vedanta Ajna is white. Ajna is the center of clarity and wisdom, the meeting point between human consciousness and divine consciousness. At this level of consciousness we can achieve Samadhi, or inspiration, where we are deeply absorbed in the spiritual. The "I" consciousness fades, and wisdom shows in all of our actions. We have a clear sense of reasoning and discrimination (Viveka) and we have overcome confusion. The mantra for Ajna is OM.

The seventh chakra is knows as the Crown chakra because it is located on the top of the head. It is called *Sahasrara*. Sahasrara is symbolized as a lotus with one thousand petals, and it is often called the center of a million rays because it radiates like the sun. There is no color to Sahasrara, it is pure brilliant light that contains all of the colors. When Sahasrara is awakened the Divine is revealed to us, and we attain Supreme Consciousness. Ignorance faces, and we have wisdom and intelligence and complete liberation, or Moksha. We have broken from the cycle of rebirth and death. The mind is still, we have reached the highest level of Samadhi where we have total spiritual absorption. The mantra for Sahasrara is the same as for Ajna, it is the original, primordial sound OM.

So, how can we help to enliven these chakras and awaken our consciousness? With spiritual practices and discipline. The success of these practices depends on both the sincerity of our practice, and the intensity and effort that we put into our practice. We need to put our whole heart into this. We need to put our emotion into this. We need to feel it. Spiritual practices are necessary because they help to prepare us for when we have our awakenings. We don't know when these awakenings are going to happen, they can't be scheduled in. They tend to be at times where we are relaxed, when we have surrendered to Spirit, and when we are ready, emotionally, mentally, spiritually and physically.

The five spiritual practices that the ancient texts recommend are:

Japa. Japa is repetition of a sacred name. This is typically done with mala beads in Eastern religions. In the Catholic tradition a rosary is used. The beads are used to count the mantras, or prayers.

Meditation. We talked about meditation earlier. There are many different kinds of meditation you can try. Vedanta says that meditation and Japa are the two most effective practices when we are striving for spiritual awakening.

Prayer. From the heart, prayer is another way to feel our connection with the Divine.

Vichara. Vichara is discriminating reasoning. It is practicing under-standing what is real and what is not real.

Pranayama. Controlled breathing exercises. This moves energy through the body.

How do we know when we are becoming awakened? True awakening begins to show up in our lives when consciousness reaches the level of the heart chakra. When this happens, emotions bubble up, and we might even cry. We get goose bumps on the skin, or feel chills. We might see lights, or auras, or hear sounds like bells ringing in the distance. Vedanta says that there are certain signs we can look for:

There is a struggle for self-control. We make an effort to subdue our outgoing sense organs. We watch what we say, and how we behave. We are thoughtful with our actions. We are careful making decisions.

We experience a great spiritual longing. We want to be awakened so much that we make it our priority. We want to know the Truth. We study, take classes, read, and focus on our spiritual practices.

We see more clearly what is Real and what is unreal. It is easy for us to see through Maya to what is Real. We become more accepting, loving, compassionate. We are also more calm and tranquil – it takes a lot more to get us upset about something.

Intense dispassion. Dispassion results in knowledge. Knowledge leads to abstention from sense pleasures. Abstention from sense pleasures leads to the experience of bliss. And the experience of bliss leads to peace.

For Further Exploration

What colors are you drawn to? What is your favorite color? Take some time today to notice all the colors of nature and how we see them express in the world.

Spend some time outside today, look up at the vastness of the sky. Feel the air on your skin. Walk barefoot in your backyard. We are connected with all of nature. Get some perspective on the meaning of this. How can we put a value on a tree? What are the many gifts that the tree gives us? How long does the tree live? The tree may live longer than we do, but it is still impermanent. What ages and stages does the tree go through? How does the tree adapt to change?

Can you feel the peace, and acceptance, and easy with which nature operates? What can you learn from nature's example?

With your eyes closed, imagine a place you would like to go. Where do you find it? Think about how you would get there, where you would stay, what you would do, what it would feel like being there. If you were planning a trip to this destination, you would know how to get there, you could physically go there given the opportunity. Now think about a spiritual or emotional "place" you would like to be – like bliss. You know where to find it, and how to get there. Be present. Observe your thoughts and emotions – don't identify with them, just watch them. Release pain. Release fear. Let go. Choose love. See our connection with nature and with each other. Be conscious. Be aware.

Have you made the choice to be happy? It's easy to be happy when things are going well. It's more difficult to be happy when things aren't going well. We need to keep making the choice, to keep checking in with ourselves and observing the thoughts and feelings that come up. Rather than identifying with these energies, allow them to pass through. Remind yourself that all of these things, the situations, the circumstances and the energies, are temporary. They come and they go. Let them go. Choose happiness; choose bliss.

Notes

Lissa Coffey

CH. 5

Living Bliss

*Let the beauty we love
be what we do.
There are a hundred ways
to kneel and kiss the ground.*

-Rumi

Vedanta talks about Truth, knowing who we are, and what is Real. How do we recognize Truth? How do we know if something is really true? There are three tests we can apply, and if something can pass all three tests, then we know that it is indeed true.

Testimony, or Scripture – Faith. In Sanskrit this is called "shruti." A wise person can tell us something, share his or her knowledge with us. Or we can read something in a book, or a spiritual text. This is the first test. Has someone else experienced it? Is there some history to this truth? Scripture or testimony on its own doesn't take away any doubt we might have.

Reason. In Sanskrit this is called "yukti." We need to use our intellect to think about whether this could be true or not. We can explore the possibility by thinking rationally. Does it make sense to us?

Vedanta says there are actually 4 types of reasoning. Vada is academic reasoning. In academics we strive to discover the Truth without bias one way or the other. Jalpa is a kind of dogmatic approach where we strive to overthrow arguments by any means, playing devil's advocate, so to speak, whether it makes sense or not. And Vitanda is the kind of reasoning that shows the flaws in an approach. It might also confuse us by presenting alternative approaches.

Rational reasoning is the type of reasoning that Vedanta recommends, and this is called Vichara. Vichara is not arguing in any way. It is not reasoning with any bias. It is simply the process of discrimination between what is real and what is unreal. This discernment is something we can practice, a skill we can hone.

Vedanta also explains that there are four disciplines we can engage to improve our reasoning skills. Discrimination, discerning the difference between what is real and what is unreal, is the first. The second is dispassion. Dispassion helps us to give up what is unreal. It helps us to overcome any emotional attachments to material objects. The third is self-control. We need self-control in order to master the mind and the senses. And the fourth is longing for liberation. How badly do we want to be free? We need to be totally devoted to the quest for Truth.

Personal experience. In Sanskrit this is called "anubhuti." There is a difference between reading something and living it. There is a difference between hearing something and having gone through the experience ourselves. This is the most convincing of the three tests.

Vedanta also goes on to say that we have three instruments of knowledge – three ways of learning what we need to learn:

Instinct. Instinct is automatic, like breathing. We don't need to think about it. At the level of instinct the "I" consciousness is dormant. Our actions are unconscious.

Reason. Reason is a mature form of instinct. At this level our actions are conscious, rather than spontaneous. We think before we act.

Intuition. Intuition is a mature form of reason. At this level our super-consciousness is engaged. This is our Higher Self speaking to us. We know things, but we don't necessarily know how we know them. It is a direct feeling of knowing. True intuition does not conflict with the experience of facts.

All of this sounds very scientific and intellectual. But there is another very important component that can't be left out. Truth can only be realized through the heart. This is where inspiration comes from. The word inspiration itself means "in spirit."

In our modern day world, as we are bombarded by information – this is the information age, and a material world where so much emphasis is placed on material things, things that are "in form" – inspiration, that of the spirit, is so important. We are starving for it.

In order to live spiritual truth we must have faith in it. Faith is much more than belief. Belief leaves some room for doubt. Faith is strong. Our spiritual quest always starts with faith, and faith is what keeps us going. Faith matures into conviction, and conviction ultimately reaches its potential in realization.

We know the Truth when we have risen above all of our beliefs. We need reason to do this. Vedanta says that we need both faith and reason together to grow into Self-knowledge. Faith comes from the heart, and reason comes from the head.

> *The fruit of silence is prayer,*
> *The fruit of prayer is faith,*
> *The fruit of faith is love and*
> *The fruit of love is silence.*
>
> *-Mother Teresa*

The Upanishads say: "Do not seek God but see him." This is asking us to see with the heart. When we seek something, it separates us from that which we are looking for. Seeking uses the head, defining something for us, and causing us to look for it outside of ourselves. But seeing is heartfelt. It is personal, a form of revelation. There is a saying that beauty is in the eye of the beholder. We see beauty because it is in us.

When we see the Truth, we don't just know it, we are it. This is a Universal Truth, true for everyone. It's the I AM statement that rings true. In Exodus 4:14 it says: "I Am That I Am." I am happy, I am blissful, I am joyful, I am free. This is who we are; this is who we are meant to be.

For Further Exploration

How strong is your instinct? What event in your life can you credit to your good instincts?

How reasonable are you? How much do you rely on your reasoning ability? Where does it serve you well?

How intuitive are you? In what ways do you use your intuition?

What does faith mean to you? Do you have faith? Do you have conviction?

What does Truth mean to you? How do you define it? How do you find it?

Finish this sentence: "I AM _____."
How does that make you feel? How True is that statement?

Notes

CH. 6

The Ayurvedic Prescription For Living a Happy Life

From time flow forth created things
From time, too, they advance in growth.
Likewise in time they disappear.
Time is a form and formless, too.

-The Upanishads

Ayurveda is the Science of Life, originating in India more than 5,000 years ago. It is a sister science with yoga and meditation. Living an ayurvedic lifestyle can be a spiritual practice in itself. There is a passage in the Caraka-Samhita, the original text that teaches us all about Ayurveda, that explains exactly how to live a happy and useful life. It makes 14 key points that we can expand on.

Those who are well wishers of all creatures, who do not aspire the wealth of others, who are truthful, peace-loving, who examine things before acting upon them, who are vigilant, who enjoy the three important desires of life without the one affecting the other, who respect superiors, who are endowed with the knowledge of arts, sciences and tranquility, who serve the elders, who have full control of passion, anger, enby, pride, and prestige, who are constantly giving to various types of charity, meditation, acquisition of knowledge, who have full knowledge of the spiritual power and are devoted to it, who make efforts both for the existing as well as the next life, and are endowed with memory and intelligence, lead a useful and happy life; others do not.

-Caraka-Samhita Sutrashtana Ch. XXX su. 24

Be a well wisher of all creatures. This means allow everyone to be happy. Be happy for other people's success. Treat all living beings with kindness. Do not cause harm, seek to alleviate suffering.

Do not aspire the wealth of others. There is no reason to be jealous. Focus on what you have, and love what you have. There is plenty of everything for everyone. You are not lacking in any way. Look at your own wealth, you have so much.

Be truthful, and peace-loving. Always be true to your word. Say what you mean, and do what you say you are going to do. See the importance of peace, and work to keep peace, or restore peace, whenever possible.

Examine things before acting up on them. Think before you speak. Look before you leap. You can't unring a bell. There are dozens of sayings that have made their way into our vernacular for a reason – they are helpful!

Be vigilant. Be strong. Have conviction. Stand up for what is right. Be true to yourself. Never give up.

Enjoy the three important desires of life (virtue, wealth, and pleasure) without the one affecting the other. Virtue is doing the right thing, for the right reason. Wealth is all the wisdom and love we have, that we can share, that goes with us after the body dies. And pleasure is the happiness and bliss that comes to us by doing good.

Respect superiors. We can learn from those who come before us. We don't have to struggle, we can learn from the experience of people who have already been there, done that.

Become endowed with the knowledge of arts, sciences, and tranquility. All three are a part of life. An important, beautiful, wonderful part of life that adds so much wonder to our experience here on earth.

Serve elders. Serve everyone, really. But elders particularly, because they have so much wisdom to offer us. We are all connected, and by helping anyone, we are also helping ourselves.

Have full control of passion, anger, envy, pride, and prestige. This doesn't say to not have these attributes. It is difficult to be devoid of them in our human existence. But we can control them. And by controlling them, we don't allow them to control us.

Give to various types of charity, meditation, acquisition of knowledge. These are ways that we can help the planet, and leave it a better place when we go. It is up to each of us to do what we can, as much as we can. We can give of our time, our treasure, or our talents.

Have full knowledge of the spiritual power and be devoted to it. Make spirituality a priority. We see the good it does in our own lives, as well as the good that it does for our community, and everyone around us. If everyone had devotion to spirituality this world would be a much happier place.

Make efforts both for the existing as well as the next life. We need to strive to learn and grow as much as we can in this life, both to make this life better, and to take with us wisdom that we can use the next time around. Our behavior matters, our actions matter, the lessons we learn matter.

Become endowed with memory and intelligence. Learn to distinguish between what is real and what is unreal. Learn to make good decisions. Remember the lessons learned so that they don't have to be repeated.

For Further Exploration

How can you express kindness today? For ideas join The Kindness Movement: EverythingKind.com

What have you learned today? Every day is an opportunity for us to learn and grow. There are options available to us including books, courses, and experiences. What wisdom has moved you with emotion today?

Who can you serve today? Who can you learn from today?

Where can you give today? Make a list of your favorite charities and non-profit organizations, and how you can help them.

Notes

CH. 7

A Grateful Heart

*If the only prayer you ever say
in your entire life is Thank You,
that would suffice.*

-Meister Eckhart

There is definitely a link between happiness and gratitude. We feel both happiness and gratitude in the heart. But which comes first? It's kind of like a "chicken and egg" dilemma. However, we can cultivate happiness by responding to the world with gratitude. It's an attitude, a spiritual attitude, which actually promotes happiness and joy. Have you noticed how great you feel when you count your blessings? We can choose to turn our attention to gratitude at any time, and bring that feeling of happiness into our awareness.

Too many times we take things, and people, for granted. We go about our day with the expectation that the alarm will ring, the water for the shower will turn on, the electricity will work with the flip of a switch, and that there will be something in the cupboard to eat for breakfast. These are little things, ordinary things, which we really don't think much about. But take them away, and suddenly we notice what we are missing. The power goes out and we are put in a tailspin! How can we go without our morning tea? Or checking our e-mail? The drama that ensues!

I heard an interesting statistic that caused me to take pause. It said that if you have all three of these things: place to live, a job, and at least one person who loves you, then you are better off than 80% of the world's population. That kind of puts things in perspective, doesn't it? We need to have gratitude for all that we have, because we have so much. We can start with being grateful for our breath, that we have another day to live. We can be grateful for our health. We can be grateful that we have shoes to put on our feet.

Gratitude is all about bringing us into present moment awareness, taking notice of what is right in front of us. And there are miracles all around us every single moment. Albert Einstein said: "There are two ways to live your life. One is as if nothing is a miracle. The other is as if everything is a miracle."

First of all, let's practice gratitude. There's an old story that Ramakrishna used to tell about an Indian holy man, a "Sadhu," whose spiritual practice was to walk to a waterfall every day. At this waterfall he would dance, sing, and praise God for the wondrous beauty he beheld. He had such enthusiasm and joy every time he saw this amazing sight. Many other people might easily have walked past that same waterfall, taking it for granted. But this Sadhu appreciated it so much, and let that appreciation fill his being with joy. What are we just walking by and missing? What happiness are we robbing ourselves of by not noticing?

We can be grateful for the people in our lives. We wouldn't be here without our parents, our grandparents, our ancestors. We may or may not have the best relationship with our parents – but it is undeniable that they are a big reason that we exist in this lifetime. It's easy to be grateful for people who have helped us over the course of our lives. We can think about our teachers, our friends, our neighbors. We know them, we trust them, they have given their time to us.

We can also be grateful to all of the people we interact with who we might not know, but who are an essential part of our lives. The mailman, the clerk at the store, the veterinarian who cares for our pets, the barista who has memorized our order, and the workers who fix the roads are all an important part of making this a happy and good place for us to live. All of this helps to remind us how we are all connected. We are here to help each other learn and grow, and we are doing that all the time. It's wonderful, and beautiful. That is something to be grateful for!

How about feeling gratitude, and appreciation, for people we may never come into contact with, who bring joy and better living to our lives? The musicians who create the songs we hear on the radio, and the architects to build our communities, and the scientists who make discoveries to improve our living conditions are all connected to us as well. What a world we live in! There is beauty and knowledge and talent all around us, which we share with each other. How can we not be grateful for that? Gratitude helps us to feel our Oneness with all that is, it shows us how we belong, and how we are a part of everything and every one. And remembering our Oneness can bring us to that state of bliss.

It's easy to feel gratitude for someone we feel has helped us, or whose work has benefited us in some way. But it's another thing to feel gratitude for someone who we don't like, who bothers us, who annoys us. What is this about? People act as mirrors for us, people act as challenges for us. This gives us opportunities to learn and to grow. We can ask ourselves why their behavior bothers us. We can learn how to respond with grace, how to turn our attention to our own behaviors.

And then what about feeling gratitude for those whom we feel have hurt us, or wronged us? The person who broke your heart, or the person who insulted you? This is more difficult. But holding ill feelings toward someone does nothing to hurt them back. It only hurts us. There's no point in holding grudges. There's no joy in that. But letting go, releasing, forgiving, and best yet, to be grateful for the experience – that allows happiness to flow in. This doesn't mean that that other person was right in what they did, it just means that you are choosing your response to what they did for your own greatest good.

The Dalai Lama said: "To be kind, honest and have positive thoughts; to forgive those who harm us and treat everyone as a friend; to help those who are suffering and never to consider ourselves superior to anyone else: even if this advice seems rather simplistic, make the effort of seeing whether by following it you can find greater happiness."

We live in a comfortable world. So we take things for granted, and tend to move towards what is comfortable and shun what is uncomfortable. But discomfort is a key component is spurring us towards change, so that we learn, and grow, and become better people. We can be grateful for our discomfort, knowing it is an opportunity for spiritual growth and a step towards the infinite happiness that we know is inevitably ours. So, while we are easily grateful for our successes, we need to also be grateful for our mistakes. These lessons in life, these trials and tribulations are a big part of the growth process. We need to remember that every-thing that has happened to us up to this point in our lives has led us to exactly where we are today. It's the joy and the sorrow, the pleasure and the pain, all of it. Swami Vivekananda said: "Glory be unto us that we have made mistakes!"

Just as everything that has happened to us in the past has led us to where we are now in the present, everything that we do in the present, will lead us to where we will be in the future. Every choice we make now will reflect on our future. So if we want things to change, we need to get out of old habits, and into new, good habits for our spiritual growth. It starts with changing our mindset, changing our thinking, taking responsibility for our own growth. And then that is followed up by making the effort, and by actually taking action.

How do we see the world? Would you consider yourself an optimist, or a pessimist? Studies have shown that optimists are happier people. Not only that, they are healthier, they have more friends, and they even live longer. In his book *Learned Optimism*, Martin Seligman, a leader in Positive Psychology, says that while some people are naturally more optimistic, optimism is a skill that can be learned. We can work on being more optimistic so that we can be happier! Do you see the glass as half-full, or half-empty? Are you looking at what you have, or what you don't have? A true optimist, even if the glass has very little in it, says: "I have water!" And if there is nothing in in that glass, says: "I have a glass!" That's gratitude.

I want to express my gratitude to you for finding this book, and for connecting with me. Everything happens for a reason. There are no coincidences. This was meant to be, and for that, I am truly grateful.

For Further Exploration

How many times have you said "thank you" today?

What are you grateful for today?

Who can you show appreciation to today?

What mistakes have you made for which you can be grateful?

Are you comfortable? In what area of your life are you uncomfortable, and how can you change that?

Are you an optimist? If so, why? If not, why not? How can you change your thinking to become more optimistic?

Notes

AFTERWORD

That is perfect. This is perfect.
Perfect comes from perfect.
Take perfect from perfect, the remainder is perfect.
May peace and peace and peace be everywhere.

-The Upanishads

Now that we have all this ancient wisdom presented before us, what do we do with it?

It's interesting that today, with all the technology at our fingertips, and all the conveniences that we have with modern living, that so many things are still a struggle for us. You'd think that all these electronics and media platforms and communications devices would make communicating easier. But in many ways it's made it more complicated. We're plugged into these appliances, but we've disconnected with each other, with nature, with spirit.

Everything happens for a reason. Everything happens exactly when it is supposed to happen. This wisdom has been around for thousands and thousands of years. And somehow, it's made its way to you today, with this book. Somehow, you are meant to know these things, at this time in your life. You are ready.

I hope this books serves as inspiration to you. Inspiration meaning in-spirit, a light that shines to illuminate the spiritual path. This is not information – we have more information that we can handle in this inform-ation age. It's not "in form" – it's not material. So many books and philosophies talk about what you can get, or can attract, or can eventually have. Vedanta, and the other eastern wisdom that I've included in this book, is really explaining to you what you are, and who you are.

But it's one thing reading about it, and one thing hearing it – it's another thing experiencing it. Faith, reason, and experience. The rest it up to you. Think about it. Practice it. Experience it. Live it. And see how you feel.

I chose the "perfect" quote above because I see perfection everywhere. There is perfection in the imperfection, and in the flaws. It's all beautiful; it's all divine. I hear so many people say there is no perfect, and that we are striving for something impossible, something that doesn't exist. How sad to look at life that way. We don't have to strive at all! We just have to see it. We just have to be.

Happiness, peace, bliss. These are gifts inside of you, covered up by conditioning, ego, societal expectations, and general clutter and noise. I hope this book helps you unwrap these gifts and indulge in what is rightfully yours. You deserve it, you've earned it, you ARE it!

Much love to you always!

Lissa

From joy I came.
For joy I live.
And in sacred joy
I shall melt again.

-Paramahansa Yogananda

ABOUT THE AUTHOR

Lissa Coffey is a lifestyle and relationship expert who serves up an inspiring blend of ancient wisdom and modern style on her website CoffeyTalk.com. She's been living an Ayurvedic lifestyle since researching her first book, "The Healthy Family Handbook," in 1996. Lissa appears frequently on television and radio and contributes to many national publications with her insightful and compassionate approach to modern-day issues. Her e-mail newsletters are enjoyed around the world by a steadily growing subscriber base. She has several e-courses available from Transformative Learning Solutions.

Lissa Coffey is a certified instructor with The Chopra Center. Deepak Chopra says: "Coffey brings the timeless wisdom of Ayurveda to a contemporary audience and shows us how to discover more about ourselves and our relationships." In 2005 she was awarded a commendation from Los Angeles Mayor Antonio Villaraigosa for her "Outstanding Contribution to the Yoga Community." In 2012 AAPNA (Association of Ayurvedic Professionals North America) awarded Lissa the "Dharma Award" for "Excellence in Promoting Awareness of Ayurveda."

To schedule Lissa as a guest on television, for a speaking engagement, or for a public appearance, visit the pressroom at CoffeyTalk.com.

OTHER TITLES BY LISSA COFFEY

The Perfect Balance Diet: 4 Weeks to a Lighter Body, Mind, Spirit & Space

What's Your Dharma: Discover the Vedic Way to Your Life's Purpose

CLOSURE and the Law of Relationship: Endings as New Beginnings

What's Your Dosha, Baby? Discover the Vedic Way for Compatibility in Life and Love

Getting There With Grace: Simple Exercises for Experiencing Joy

Getting There! 9 Ways to Help Your Kids Learn What Matters Most in Life

The Healthy Family Handbook: Natural Remedies for Parents and Children (co-authored with Louise Taylor)

Freddy Bear's Wakeful Winter

Feng Shui For Everyday: Easy Ways to Bring Abundance Into Your Home and Workplace

ACKNOWLEDGEMENTS

Everything I've been through up to this point brought me to where I am today. And for that I am grateful. I am been fortunate to have had amazing teachers. Thank you Deepak Chopra, Vasant Lad, Louise Taylor, and Swami Kriyananda. I continue to be inspired by you and your work. Thank you to Dr. Suhas Kshirsagar, a friend and mentor to me. We share a passion for Ayurveda and Vedic philosophy and for bringing this important information to a greater audience here in the west.

Thank you to the very talented McKenzie Bateman for the beautiful cover art created just for this book. McKenzie is beautiful inside and out and it shows in her work.

Much love and gratitude goes to both my family and to my global family. We're all in this together, and your support and encouragement mean the world to me. You inspire me! And my wonderful husband Greg: Thank you for truly being my partner in this journey. You keep me laughing, and I love you more every single day.

My CoffeyTalk team gets bouquets of gratitude from me: Ophelia, Jon, Eric, and Ray, you are the BEST. And a special thank you goes to the amazing and talented team at Transformative Learning Solutions, especially Rishabh and Venu.

GLOSSARY OF SANSKRIT WORDS AND TERMS

Agni: Fire

Ahimsa: Non-violence, non-harmfulness in thought, word, and deed.

Akash: Space

Ajna: The third eye chakra

Anahata: The heart chakra.

Ananda: Bliss

Anandakanda: The root of bliss, represented as a lotus in the heart center.

Anandamaya Kosha: The fifth layer of the body, closest to the Real Self. Bliss.

Annamaya Kosha: The outermost layer that covers the body.

Anubhuti: Personal experience.

Apas: Water

Artha: Prosperity, wealth, acquisition of wealth.

Asana: This is the third of the eight steps in Raja Yoga. Perfect balance. Postures.

Ayurveda: India's "Science of Life."

Bhakta: One who practices Bhakti Yoga.

Bhakti Yoga: The path of love.

Chakra: Centers of spiritual consciousness

Dasya: Loving God as a master.

Dharana: This is the sixth of the eight steps in Raja Yoga. Concentration.

Dharma: Purpose, duty, truth. Also, righteous conduct.

Dhyana: This is the seventh of the eight steps in Raja Yoga. Meditation.

Gunas: Qualities.

Guru: A spiritual teacher.

Hari: One of the Sanskrit names for God, one who attracts all things.

Japa: Repetition of the sacred name.

Jivanmukti: Liberation, freedom while living in the body.

Jnana Yoga: The path of knowledge.

Jnani: One who practices Jnana Yoga.

Kama: Pleasure. The fulfillment of legitimate desires.
Karma: Work, action, and the effects of that work or action. Also, habit.
Karma Yoga: The path of work.
Kosha: Layer, sheath.
Kundalini: spiritual power

Madhura: Loving God as our beloved.
Manipura: The solar plexus chakra.
Manomaya Kosha: The third layer of the body, the mind.
Mantra: Sanskrit syllables or sounds that combine into sacred words. Instrument of the mind. A tool used during meditation.
Maya: Illusion.
Moksha: Liberation, freedom of the soul.
Muladhara: The root chakra.

Namaste: Sanskrit greeting: "The divine in me honors the divine in you."
Niyama: This is the second of the eight steps of Raja Yoga. Discipline.

Om: A mantra in itself. Represents Oneness, the Universal.

Paramatman: The Self, the Soul.
Patanjali: Author of the Yoga Sutras, the text of Raja Yoga.
Prana: Life force. Breath. Energy
Pranayama: This is the fourth of the eight steps in Raja Yoga. The control of the life force, controlled energy. Also, controlled breathing exercises.
Pranayama Kosha: The second layer, what animates us, the vital force.
Pratyahara: This is the fifth of the eight steps in Raja Yoga. The control of the senses, self-restraint.
Prithvi: Earth

Rajas: One of the three gunas. The quality of overactivity.
Raja Yoga: The path of meditation.
Rishi: A scholar, sage.

Sahasrara: The crown chakra.
Sakhya: Loving God as a friend.
Samadhi: This is the final step in the eight steps in Raja Yoga. Absolute bliss. Experiencing Oneness.
Samskara: Mental impressions, habits that make up our character.
Samyama: The last three steps in Raja Yoga practiced together: Dharana, Dhayana and Samadhi.

Santa: Peaceful loving.
Sattva: One of the three gunas. The quality of balance, calm.
Seva: Selfless service
Shruti: Scripture, testimony, or faith.
Sutra: Stitch, stitch of knowledge.
Svadhistana: The sacral chakra
Swasthya: Established in oneself.

Tamas: One of the three gunas. The quality of inactivity, sluggishness.
Turiya: The omnipresent consciousness, being.

Vatsalya: Loving God as our child.
Vayu: Air
Vichara: Discriminating reasoning.
Vijnanamaya Kosha: The fourth layer of the body, the intellect.
Visudda: The throat chakra.
Viveka: Discrimination.

Yama: The first of the eight steps in Raja Yoga. Truthfulness, nonviolence.
Yoga: To unite, union.
Yogi: One who practices Yoga.
Yukti: Reason.

REFERENCES AND
RECOMMENDED READING

Adiswaranda, Swami. "The Vedanta Way to Peace and Happiness"
SkyLight Paths, 2007

Ashley-Farrand, Thomas, "Healing Mantras: Using Sound Affirmations for
Personal Power, Creativity, and Healing"
Ballantine-Wellspring, New York, NY, 1999

Chopra, Deepak. "The Ultimate Happiness Prescription: 7 Keys to Joy and
Enlightenment"
Harmony, 2009

Eknath Easwaran (Translator), "The Upanishads (Classic Indian Spirituality)
Nilgiri Press, 2007

Hospodar, Miriam Kasin, "Heaven's Banquet: Vegetarian Cooking for Life-
long Health the Ayurveda Way"
Dutton, New York, NY, 1999
Iyengar, B.K.S., "Light on Pranayama: The Yogic Art of Breathing"
Crossroad Publishing Company, New York, NY, 2002

Khalsa, M.D., Dharma Singh, and Stauth, Cameron, "Meditation as Medicine: Activate the Power of Your Natural Healing Force"
Pocket Books, New York, NY, 2001

Kshirsagar, Suhas G., "The Hot Belly Diet"
Atria Books, 2014

Lad, Vasant, ""Textbook of Ayurveda: Fundamental Principles"
The Ayurvedic Press, 2002

Pert, Candace, "Molecules of Emotion: The Science Behind Mind-Body
Medicine"
Simon & Schuster, 1999

Prabhupada, Srila, "The Higher Taste: A Guide to Gourmet Vegetarian Cooking and a Karma –Free Diet"
The Bhaktivedanta Book Trust, Los Angeles, CA, 2006

Prabhupada, A.C. Bhaktivedanta Swami, "Bhagavad-Gita: As It Is"
The Bhaktivedanta Book Trust, 1997

Saraswati, Sri Chandrasekharendra, "The Vedas"
Bhavan's Book University, 2009

Schäfer, Lothar, "Infinite Potential: What Quantum Physics Reveals About How We Should Live"
Deepak Chopra, 2013

Vivekananda, Swami. "Vedanta: Voice of Freedom."
St. Louis, MO: Vedanta Society of St. Louis, 1986

Vrajaprana, Pravajika, "Vedanta: A Simple Introduction"
Vedanta Press and Bookshop, 1999

RESOURCES

The Ayurvedic Balance Diet Club
www.perfectbalancediet.com
Menus, recipes, videos, meditations and more!

DharmaSmart: Purposeful Living Essentials
www.DharmaSmart.com
Ayurvedic remedies, oils, herbs and more!

Letters To Lissa www.CoffeyTalk.com
What's Your Dosha? Quiz and more www.WhatsYourDosha.com
What's Your Dharma? Your Life Purpose www.WhatsYourDharma.com
All About Meditation www.PSMeditation.com
Dosha Design: Vastu & Feng Shui www.DoshaDesign.com
Sleep Tips www.BetterSleep.org
The Ayurveda Experience www.AyurvedaECourse.com
The Kindness Movement www.EverythingKind.com

Social Media
YouTube.com/coffeytalk
Facebook.com/lissacoffeytalk
Twitter.com/coffeytalk
Instagram.com/lissacoffey
Pinterest.com/lissa_coffey
HuffingtonPost.com/lissa-coffey

Notes